PERFECT
ENGAGEMENT

D1157716

A practical guide to a more dynamic Rotary Club

Donna Hernandez • Lori Fickling • Mike Fickling

PERFECT ENGAGEMENT
A practical guide to a more dynamic Rotary Club

Co-Authors: Donna Hernandez, Lori Fickling &
Mike Fickling

FIRST EDITION

Library of Congress Control Number: 2018946524

Published by: Adriel Publishing

Co-Published by: Perfect Engagement Publishing LLC

Printed in the United States of America

ISBN: 978-1-892324-03-0

www.PerfectEngagementPublishing.com

DEDICATION

Perfect Engagement: A practical guide to a more dynamic Rotary Club is dedicated to the 62 charter members of the Cross Timbers Rotary Club:

Andy Eads	Paul Frederiksen	Fred Placke
Lori Fickling	Phil Geleske	Nate Prevost
Ginger Eads	Rhonda Godbey	Tricia Robinson
Lori Walker	Lisa Goocher	Jim Rosengren
Chuck Elsey	Teresa Grawe	Aaron Rosengren
Julie Meyer	Jeri Harwell	Lori Salisbury
LaSharndra Barbarin	David Henry	Dana Smith
Brandi Bird	Donna Hernandez	Dawn Sprayman
Robert Bird	Tom Heslep	Tyler Sprayman
Matt Brost	David Hodges	Dan Staples
Matthew Bryan	Steve Holzwarth	Jimmy Stathatos
Will Carlton	Mary Jones	Rusty Sullivan
Cheryl Close	Carol Kyer	Scott Tarwater
Kevin Corprew	Marianne Lagerstrom	Donna Tarwater
Dianne Costa	Connie Miller	Kay Trotter
Shelly Dodge	Jim Moll	Spencer Turner
Tracee Elrod	Alison Mosely	Neal Walker
Kristin Feeback	Tony Mowles	Russell Webb
Tommy Fellers	Les Nasche	Kris Wise
Mike Fickling	Debbie Nelson	Mary Worthington
Al Filidoro	Lisa Pierce-Johnson	

PREFACE

We were first made aware of the idea of Perfect Engagement by our friend Gerald Robinson, who is now the incoming District Governor of Rotary District 5790. This concept was shared at a Rotary leadership training conference and he was enthusiastic about how it could change Rotary for the better.

Earlier this year, after posting a photo on Facebook with some of my fellow Cross Timbers Rotarians, I received a Facebook private message from a Rotary International District Governor Elect asking whether our club had a webinar or video about how to set up a new club that we could share with others. He told me about a club that had received a charter but explained how they had let the charter expire because of differences among the founders' concepts, such as sticking with Rotary tradition versus incorporating new ideas. He was interested in our club's discussions regarding dues, meetings, etc. that carved out the direction that we eventually took in forming the Cross Timbers Rotary Club.

At this same time, as a part of the completion of my graduate studies in Strategic Communication and Innovation from Texas Tech University, I was conducting research and writing a master's report on communications issues within service organizations and the Cross Timbers Rotary Club in particular. I found that while there are a few reference books about Rotary International and membership in service organizations, there is little current information about how to make Rotary Clubs engaging and relevant to members in this fast-paced electronic era of social networking.

With that, the idea for this book was conceived. I immediately turned to my long-time friends, Lori and Mike Fickling, each of whom had often discussed writing a book about Rotary with me. In the late 1990s, the three of us had created and co-owned a local newspaper that we ultimately sold to the Fort Worth Star-Telegram in 2005. Luckily, the Ficklings were up for the challenge and agreed to make this book a reality.

We understand that each Rotary Club must be true to its members and embrace its own values, traditions and culture. Through our suggestions, we are not trying to persuade that our way of doing things is the only way, or even the best way. But rather our goal is to share with you some of the philosophies and activities that have worked for our organization and to explain how *Perfect Engagement* makes us look forward to Friday morning Rotary meetings and each of our social and service group meetings that have grown out of our fellowship at Rotary.

– Donna Hernandez

TABLE OF CONTENTS

CHAPTER 1

The Case for Rotary

"Alone we can do so little; together we can do so much."
– Helen Keller

What's the appeal of joining an organization that started in the early 1900's? What could a turn-of-the-century service and networking club possibly offer in the 21st century? How could the ideals and beliefs on which it was founded be relevant today?

A larger question to consider is, why do people join service organizations in the first place? What attracts millions of people around the globe to gather with others to serve? And what draws them to one group over another?

Let's look at this phenomenon.

Almost everyone has a desire to make the world a better place. Admittedly, some feel this desire more than others, while some prefer to work alone and only occasionally. But rare is the person who doesn't care at all.

So, what does Rotary International do for this common desire to do good in the world?

Rotary gives each person a place to serve where they can truly make a difference. Rotary puts individuals together with like-minded people, which increases the effect exponentially. Suddenly, the efforts in a community are multiplied and the impact is widespread.

In addition, Rotary connects its local clubs to the needs of the world. The ability to take on water projects, literacy efforts, disease eradication, and many other causes suddenly becomes reality. No longer does success rest with one person, or even with one club, but instead takes on global significance when paired with clubs from around the world.

To add to the impact, individuals are not dependent on simply the amount of money they can contribute, but rather on fundraising efforts enhanced by the organization of Rotary and the Rotary Foundation. A dollar given today turns into several dollars in the near future.

An ancillary benefit to joining Rotary, over and above the service aspect, is the bond of friendship and fellowship of family gained through working on service projects alongside fellow club members.

Planting flowers at the local shelter for homeless teens, pouring wine at an event that raises money to stop child abuse, or sorting women's business clothes to organize the interview closet at a women's shelter breaks down all barriers and creates instant friendships.

Joining a local Rotary Club provides individuals the opportunity to create lasting and positive change, both in the local community and around the world. Membership in Rotary reminds us that the world is bigger than just our immediate family and friends and provides an opportunity to broaden our horizons and think globally, as well as locally.

A popular question to ask oneself now is "What's My Why?"

When Simon Sinek began exploring the concept of *"start with your why,"* he changed the way we all talk about our motivations, our passions and what drives us. He tells us to first dig deep and that *"it's those who start with WHY that have the ability to inspire those around them."*

When we ask people what it is about Rotary they love, and what keeps them committed to Rotary membership, members have many "whys." Here are a few we encountered:

"I enjoy the fellowship with like-minded people."

***

"I have a desire and a need to serve."

***

"The bond of friendship with club members is priceless."

***

"We connect to projects in other countries that change lives."

***

"I love volunteering with friends."

***

"It's an uplifting way to start the day."

***

"This is an opportunity to make a difference in lives of local youth."

The answers may vary, but the underlying truth is the same: Rotary offers people of all ages an outlet for their desire to do good. It gives us community.

What other group can you be a part of that will welcome you to any meeting in any country in the world?

What other group can you be a part of that enables you to supply a mobile medical clinic to a previously unserved remote village in Kenya?

What other group can you be a part of that opens the door to host an exchange student for a year and build a relationship that lasts a lifetime?

14

What other group can you be a part of that brings the gift of clean water to people who otherwise would have no access to it?

What other group can you be a part of that puts hands and feet into action to help bring mobile showers to a city's homeless population to restore them a little dignity?

What other group can you be a part of that sets its mind to eradicating a disease – and does it?!

Being a member of your local Rotary club is the start of an adventure! Suddenly you are part of 1.2 million others like yourself who regularly gather in meetings in more than 200 countries across the world.

This quote from Helen Keller expresses perfectly the power of Rotary.

**"Alone we can do so little;
together we can do so much."**

Being a member of your local Rotary club is the start of a wonderful journey!

Rotary's motto, **"Service Above Self,"** reminds us that *we* are not the focus, but rather our *service to others*.

So, is an organization founded in 1905 still relevant today? Can we apply the founding principles of Rotary to make our community and our world a better place?

We offer a resounding YES!

CHAPTER 2

Rethinking Your Club - It's Always The Right Time

"If you always do what you've always done, you'll always get what you've always got."
– Henry Ford

Once upon a time there was a Rotary club preparing to celebrate its 100th anniversary. This club was steeped in tradition, which was comforting to many of its members, but every week the meeting was conducted in exactly the same manner it always had been. The membership of the club was steady – not increasing but not decreasing.

The problem was that no new ideas or changes had been implemented in decades. Club members had begun to dread going to the meetings week after week, and their enthusiasm and interest was fading.

So what happened?

It's pretty easy to get comfortable and lulled into a routine. In fact, it's human nature. We shouldn't expect that to be any different where Rotary is concerned. But what we must guard against at every turn is the possibility of our club growing stale.

We offer this encouragement often – because we believe it strongly: *If you don't enjoy your Rotary club meeting as much or more as almost anything else you do in a week, it's time to reevaluate your club.*

The prospect of starting a new Rotary club, or anything new, is exciting and challenging, and quite honestly a great deal of fun. These same principles, however, can be applied to rethinking what you already have, especially a Rotary club that's been in existence for a while.

Then it's time to rethink your club!

So what does that mean exactly? Let's start with assessing your strengths and weaknesses. It sounds cliché, but this is a necessary step. So how do we go about this process?

Ask yourself these questions:

1. **What do we do well as a club?**

   Think of projects and events where everything seems to click. Members are happy, the results are positive, and your club is known to do this well. This is a strength – capitalize on it!

2. As a Rotary club, where do we fall short?

Do your members turn their nose up at service projects? Would they rather write a check than get their hands dirty? Do you have infighting among your members? Think of the three biggest issues that keep you from being an effective Rotary club. Gather two or three other members and begin to tackle the problems. Often these issues are not easy to solve, but refer to the section below on turning around unhappy members and begin to build support for change.

3. What do we want to be known for?

Some Rotary clubs are known for their Foundation giving. Some Rotary clubs are known for doing service projects every month. Some Rotary clubs are known for being friendly and generous. Decide on your club's identity and spend your time developing it to its fullest. You might consider going through Rotary's visioning process as a club to help in identifying your priorities. This will also help you begin to spend *less* time on the things that don't fit your club's mission and goals.

4. What holds us back and keeps us from being a successful Rotary club?

It's time for a little honest introspection. Take a hard look at the roadblocks – and the people – that stand in the way of progress and success.

Write these down and print them out or use a flip chart so you can really get clear on the answers and what steps to take next, as well as who will take the action.

In addition to assessing your strengths and weaknesses, let's look at your members. Dealing with unhappy members can be tricky, but here are a few tips to get them turned around:

1. **Identify disgruntled members.**
   Do you have members who never seem to be happy with anything your club is doing? Does their constant complaining affect your other members? Do they object to every new idea? When you identify these members, you have taken the first step toward solving this problem.

2. **Put your enthusiastic members to work as peacemakers.**
   A little understanding can go a long way in Rotary – and in life. It's hard to be angry with someone who approaches you in a spirit of kindness and understanding. Use your Rotary "cheerleaders" and ambassadors to soften your complacent or unhappy members.

3. **Listen.**

   Really listen to your members, especially the ones who are not happy. Sometimes the simple act of listening can assure a person they are being heard and goes a long way to diffuse a heated situation. In addition, this method gets them involved in the solution. And bonus: you will learn a few things about how your club is perceived in the process.

4. **Explain your motives.**

   Once the problem member knows your intentions – that they are purely motivated and for the good of everyone – they are much more likely to become a supporter, and maybe even a part of the team.

5. **Give them a job.**

   As we discuss in another chapter, break down your club's tasks into small jobs and assign everyone to something – preferably something they have an interest in or do well. If every member takes ownership of something, no matter how big or how small, their attitude will change from one of criticism to one of enthusiasm and support.

When going through the process of rethinking your club, take advantage of the resources provided by Rotary International. Rotary is now offering several creative options for membership, including associate memberships, corporate memberships, family memberships and others. Be sure and check out the new series in the Rotarian magazine called "Club Innovation" for updates and ideas to bring your club into the 21st century.

Remember, every club has its own special club culture. Club culture and characteristics are developed over many years and ultimately become tradition. Club cultures and traditions are not good or bad, just different. You've heard the old line, *"If it ain't broke, don't fix it."* While that is true, if you find your club has lost some of its charm, don't hesitate to shake it up a bit!

What are you doing to rethink your club?

CHAPTER 3

Effective Member Recruitment & Retention – Relationships Are Key

"People rarely succeed unless they find fun in what they are doing."
– Dale Carnegie

If you have ever publicly encouraged reaching for the phone book or turning to online business listings to resolve your recruiting needs – STOP. You need a better plan!

The recruitment of quality prospects and the retention of valuable members is far too crucial to the growth and success of a club, and it deserves your full attention and a definitive plan. It's also a great opportunity to reflect on the core values and attributes that have defined Rotarians for well over a hundred years.

Start by looking for prospects who have a giving heart and a burning desire to serve others – a person with proven character and integrity.

How about starting with the most complete database you could ever have and one you carry with you everywhere you go? Yes, consider opening your smart phone and looking through your contacts. Then ask yourself, "Who would I enjoy having lunch with or breakfast or drinks?"

Imagine taking 10 minutes during a regular meeting and encouraging every member to consider the friends and associates they are already connected to. *Take out your phones and make a list – GO!*

Here are a few tips:

1. Identify three people you would like to learn more about. Maybe someone from another country or culture. Maybe the young mother from your neighborhood whose children are now in school and has some new-found time to commit to helping others. It might even be a new business owner in town who mentioned she was a Rotarian in her

home town but has simply not been invited since moving.

2. Don't overlook the obvious. How many couples belong to your club? Consider a known entity like your spouse or your best friend as a potential new member.

3. Seek out people who are well known in your community: members of the chamber of commerce, doctors, accountants, lawyers, or city officials.

4. Recruit with a purpose, not a net. It is every member's obligation to network with new members in mind.

5. Avoid recruiting through the classifieds, or holding a "membership roundup" or "new member month." Keep it personal and make it *intentional*. And remember, being more selective builds a club membership of influencers and people who can "get things done."

6. It's easy to build your membership when everyone is invited to simply "come have *FUN* with us!" Don't get this wrong – we love FUN – but not as the *primary* reason to involve new members.

A quick note on extending a proper invitation. It must be obvious to your friend that the invitation is sincere and important to you, and it ***must*** be done face to face, preferably over lunch or coffee. This is not an action that can be done in a group text or a word in passing. Your guests should feel genuinely honored you chose them and took the time to tell them about Rotary and what it means to you.

Retention

It must be said that the retention rate of any club starts with recruiting the right candidates, period.

Nothing is more frustrating than gaining two fantastic members and losing four "family" members at the same meeting. This is all the more frustrating when the losses come as a complete surprise to those who remain.

Rotary, we have a problem.

If a member missed a meeting last month, then a couple more this month, and eventually disappears completely, only to send a note thirty days later informing you they are "leaving the club, love you guys," stop what you are doing and address the problem immediately.

Surely your club policies outline a serious exit interview to avoid the surprises every time a member leaves, right? If you want to avoid losing several additional members during the next six months, it is essential to take an honest assessment of what might have happened and what you as a club can do to address any issues that might have developed. The operative word here is *"honest."*

Nothing can damage a membership as much as a "family" Rotarian leaving and the club appearing to not notice, or not miss them, or worse, seeming to not care.

Did they just get bored? Or apathetic? Overlooked or overwhelmed? Maybe they took a new job that transferred them, or another unavoidable reason. Maybe the member is in need of help or support from a close friend and Rotarian.

Retention is usually the direct product of engagement. Every member needs to be engaged with the membership, as well as the activities, to the point they feel needed, important and comfortable. They need to retain the passion for their service and the relationships they have built from within the club membership.

There are some important things a club can do to affect the overall level of interest and passion of the members on a regular basis.

For example, how would you rate the programs of your club over the past six months? Twenty-four programs; how many of them were great? How many of them were a total waste of your time? Be honest. If twenty of them would not be considered by a majority of the membership as "really good" or "great," you might need to place more emphasis on and spend more time planning the programs.

The member or committee chair responsible for scheduling the programs needs to be a clearly designated individual who is highly organized, outgoing, meticulous, involved, and knowledgeable about the community and the people who live and work there. It is a huge responsibility and it does more than most of the other things your club will do to create interest and shape the personality of the entire membership.

We highly recommend a designated coordinator rather than a "program by committee" or a rotating scheduler system. This is, in part, due to having only one definitive calendar to manage by one definitive administrator. The entire membership can communicate any and all referrals of quality speakers or programs they encounter to the coordinator. This ensures consistency and reduces miscommunications and duplications.

Inspiring and relevant programs create interest and reduce apathy, and are a powerful tool for retaining members. Besides, everyone wants to be "glad they came today."

Equally important to membership retention are the club fellowships, or special interest social groups, that organically grow from a vibrant and active club. Members should be encouraged to share their social interests, hobbies and passions. This is a wonderful way to develop personal relationships with a smaller, intimate group of friends who have common interests.

Some popular fellowships include: book readers club, wine fellowship, cooking or dining club, cards or dominoes players, gardeners, campers, cruisers, movie buffs, theatre lovers, pet owners or car clubs, just to name a few. It is easy to have fun with as few as four participants when you are doing an activity you are passionate about. The more personal the relationships, the stronger the membership.

Finally, it has been suggested that Rotary promote member retention by making a change to the Rotary Four-Way Test.

Relax – if you're reading this and feeling a bit faint at the very notion of such sacrilege, have no fear. The suggested change is to simply add a fifth "unofficial" test, with the fifth question being: WILL IT BE FUN?

CHAPTER 4

Time, Talent, Treasure – It All Matters

"The meaning of life is to find your gift, the purpose of life is to give it away."
– Joy J. Golliver

The recruitment, development and retention of Rotarians to ensure success into the future depends on attracting quality members from the widest possible cross section of our communities. There must be a place for everyone to contribute in a way that makes them feel welcome, important and comfortable.

If you recruit deliberately and invite members who are already active in the community, your membership will be made up of seasoned professionals who may be extremely busy with their own business of making a living, raising a family, participating in other civic or charitable organizations and being a positive influence on the community.

Let's look at how to get the best of all worlds.

It is often said when being a part of a group or organization, everyone has one or more of these assets to offer: Time, Talent, or Treasure. Most members contribute a combination of the three naturally, but everyone must feel their unique contributions are important and valuable to the overall success of their club, no matter which of these three is their strength.

Time

While it takes monetary donations combined with a variety of skills and talents to make a successful, well-rounded Rotary club, we must give credit to those who have time on their hands and love to get involved in projects.

These are the members who help set up fundraising events, mentor at the local school, gather donations for an upcoming service project, coordinate volunteers and make sure nothing slips through the cracks, and so much more. To say it would be impossible to have a successful Rotary club without members who have the time to commit to its success would be an understatement. If your gift is time, Rotary is the perfect place for you.

While all Rotarians are required to make a commitment of their personal time, naturally, some have more to offer than others. It takes time to attend the meetings to discuss and act on the business of the club on a weekly basis, but it's a crucial element to a club's success and growth.

Time is also required to plan, organize and host fundraising events, to attend important functions and training, for participation at district conferences and social events, volunteering for service projects, attending international conventions, and so on.

This is especially true of those Rotarians who aspire to be a part of the leadership of their clubs as board members, committee chairpersons or officers. It takes a significant commitment of time to be an active member and to develop skills and gain experience that will ultimately benefit the entire club.

While this commitment of time is critical to the success of Rotary, it must be pointed out that this is not the only consideration. We will continue to miss out on some of the most qualified and successful Rotary candidates unless we shift our thinking on the "time" requirement and consider ways to get these leaders involved.

Which brings us to "Talent."

Talent

Another significant contribution to a Rotary club are the talents of prospective members that would directly benefit the club.

Corporate CEOs, local and state office holders, traveling sales professionals, and a host of other large groups of community leaders are inherently disqualified from the most influential service organization in the world because of a long-held, often impractical, demand on their time.

This is often to the detriment of Rotary International.

Obviously, these leaders have tremendous talent and could make valuable members, enhancing the organization and community service goals of any club, yet it's amazing how many times they are overlooked simply because we assume they are too busy. How sad that we might never have the opportunity to tap into their talents.

To take advantage of a member who has talent to offer but might be short on time, we must be more willing to extend a personal invitation and not worry so much about what their attendance percentage will be. We can offer them the chance to multiply their individual talents by joining with an organization that serves the community and the world.

It is worth mentioning here that there are also a multitude of quality, talented candidates who experience life changes every year that may make them available to be a part of a local Rotary club. People retire with talents that are invaluable to a club and they are naturally reconsidering the best use of newfound free time that was never available to them during their working years. Teachers, police officers, firefighters and nurses, for example, have talents and experience working with children and the elderly and often are looking for a way to plug into the community and continue to use their talent for good.

Rotary needs members with talent, so let's not overlook the talent that is right in front of us. Often that person is just waiting on an invitation, and it's our job to ask!

Treasure

Admittedly, Rotarians come from all walks of life and, as we've discussed, each brings something different to the club. Not all can give large sums of money, even to causes they are passionate about.

But many do.

This brings us to our third critical attribute – Treasure. There are many potential members that can contribute unique treasures or possessions to the mission of Rotary. A successful business owner looking to invest money back into the health and welfare of his community may simply need to know the mission and goals of your club for his consideration.

Many of the most qualified and committed prospects for Rotary have professional demands on their time that simply will not allow them to be at every weekly meeting. But if Rotary is to grow and thrive in the future, it is imperative that we understand and adjust our thinking so as not to disqualify these prospects based solely on their time limitations.

The last thing you want to do is to alienate him or her simply because they can't be at every meeting. Don't make the mistake of penalizing or disregarding a wealthy member who travels for business just because you don't see them as often as you like. Instead, just know their participation falls under the heading of "Treasure," and there is a place for them in Rotary.

Wouldn't it be great to have a member who is the owner/ manager of a hotel or large restaurant or other facility that could host a banquet or fundraising event? How about a local chef that would donate their services for your next banquet in exchange for the exposure it could bring to his business?

Are they a member of your club?

Imagine the impact of a local medical supply business or association that would readily donate an ambulance or medical equipment to a Rotary project to serve several villages who currently have no medical care at all. This synergy is invaluable and has profound effects that are felt world-wide. In fact, it "builds good will and better friendships" and is "beneficial to all concerned."

Get them involved with an appropriate invitation and put aside the "perfect attendance" string that is holding you back, and instead focus on "perfect engagement."

Let's face it, we can't be effective in our community or in the world without the funds to take on worthwhile projects that will help us achieve our goals and meet the needs, both locally and abroad. We need those members whose asset is Treasure!

These three attributes – Time, Talent, Treasure – do not preclude members being chosen according to the core values and mission of Rotary as written over one hundred years ago. Friendship and a true heart for helping people at home and around the world is still essential to the long-term success of the organization.

CHAPTER 5

Getting Women in the Game – A Long Time Coming

"In the future there will be no female leaders.
There will just be leaders."

– Sheryl Sandberg

For over a hundred years, Rotary has proven to be one of the most successful service organizations in the world. If there is a single criticism to be found, it would certainly be that it can be slow to accept and institute change.

One of the five explicit core values of Rotary International is to promote diversity, yet women account for less than 20 percent of its membership worldwide.

For decades now, Rotary International has discussed the immediate need to recruit both younger members and female members if they expect to survive and be relevant for the next century. Speakers from around the world have hosted countless breakout sessions at international conventions calling for immediate and affirmative action of the leadership and members at large to address the age and gender imbalance.

Increasing the number of women among its membership is one of Rotary International's primary objectives in the coming years. Rotary members participate in more than 35,000 clubs in over 200 countries to promote peace, fight disease, support education and help grow local economies, yet still the presence of women is sorely lacking.

Chicago attorney Paul Harris formed the first Rotary Club in 1905 so that professionals with diverse backgrounds could come together on a weekly basis to make friends, discuss ideas, network and contribute to the good of their community. He deliberately targeted *men* in business, in keeping with the social norms of the time.

Rotary was an instant success and within sixteen years clubs had been founded on six continents. A Rotary Club in New York was instrumental in the formation of the United Nations, and today, Rotary International is the only non-governmental organization that holds a seat at the United Nations.

Despite the success and prestige afforded Rotary International, proposals to admit women into the membership failed in the 1960s and 1970s, with one Rotary Club in Duarte, California, even losing its charter after admitting women in 1977, in contradiction of the Standard Rotary Club Constitution. The Duarte club filed a lawsuit against Rotary International and, after several appeals, on May 4, 1987, the

United States Supreme Court ruled that Rotary clubs may not exclude women from membership based solely on their sex.

In 1989, because of the Supreme Court ruling, the Rotary International Constitution was amended to welcome women members around the world and as a result, the Duarte club inducted the first woman club president. In 2017, Rotarians celebrated the 30th anniversary of women in Rotary.

It's surprising that now, well into the 21st century, we are still talking about how to get more women into Rotary – but we are. After three decades of women's participation in Rotary International, the percentage of women members in the United States, Caribbean Islands and Canada is about 26 percent, while the percentage of women members worldwide is only 19 percent.

The Rotary International 2013 Regional Membership Supplement says,

> *"Attracting more women members is a major factor to ensure Rotary's future. Women have long proven their worth at the community and international level, leading in a multitude of professions and excelling at the highest professional level."*

In his address to the 2017 Rotary International Convention, incoming 2017-2018 Rotary International President Elect, Ian Riseley, said one of the two most important challenges to be addressed by the organization in the coming years is the *"gender imbalance in the membership."*

In the President-Elect's address, he said, *"It has been twenty-eight years since our Council on Legislation voted, in a decision that was long overdue, to admit women to membership in Rotary. Twenty-eight years on, the percentage of women serving in our clubs is only just over 20 percent. That's up from about 13 percent ten years ago. At that rate, it will take us another three decades to get to where we should be: full gender parity, with as many women in Rotary clubs as men."*

Three decades is far too long to wait to achieve a Rotary that reflects the world in which we live. We need to make it a priority now.

So, you are convinced that you need more women in your club. Now let's talk about how we can accomplish that goal.

1. Membership in a Rotary Club is by invitation of existing members so, invite women! Seek out women in the community that exemplify Rotary's core values and welcome them into the club.

2. Openly discuss financial, cultural and gender impediments to women joining your club.

3. Be sensitive to time constraints. Many women work full time while raising a family or caring for elderly parents, which limits there time for participation in club events.

4. Recognize that cultural differences can restrict successful communications efforts in today's multi-cultural global community. Don't assume that a campaign to recruit more women into membership ranks will take the same shape in every club or every culture. Instead, embrace those cultural differences.

5. Create a specific strategic plan to overcome the barriers to female membership established over hundreds of years.

6. Brainstorm with existing Rotarians about their concerns about including more women in their club. Learn what Rotarians think are barriers to more women members so that those issues can be incorporated into future messages.

7. Consider a contest among area clubs with awards and recognition for increasing the percentage of women within their clubs.

The ultimate objective is to mentor a local cultural shift in the ideology of Rotarians – one club and one member at a time. With a little effort, clubs can eliminate the barriers to women's entry into membership and opportunities for success by offering encouragement and support for both existing male members and new women members. Education and mentorship are the key.

Membership in Rotary comes with many benefits for women, including the ability to fellowship with other professionals from diverse backgrounds, ethnicities and religions. Connections with other professionals extend beyond borders.

Women are afforded the opportunity to expand their social and professional network and to gain valuable leadership skills, while at the same time giving back to their community and to less advantaged communities around the globe.

Women are not asking for, or expecting, a change to the core values of the organization or the lowering of standards simply to increase their numbers, but rather action on the club leadership level to make clubs more appealing to those women who, like their male counterparts, deserve consideration.

Email us at letstalk@PerfertEngagementPublishing.com if you have questions about including women in your Rotary club.

CHAPTER 6

Let's Talk About Diversity – Refining Your Membership

"In diversity there is beauty and there is strength."
– Maya Angelou

Stephen Covey says, *"Strength lies in differences, not in similarities."* We like to think that with these few short words, Covey reminds us that when we are all the same our efforts are limited, but when we celebrate our differences we are strong beyond what we could ever imagine.

One of the most difficult assignments a Rotary club can realize is that of building a strong core of cultural diversity into its membership. We can site dozens of research projects that have determined the long-term benefits of creating and growing an organization rich in cultural diversity, but the difficult truth is the issue has been discussed for decades by clubs from around the world with only marginal results.

To address the elephant in the room, we must ask ourselves, "Why can we not, despite years of our best efforts, solve a seemingly simple challenge? How do we build a club that truly reflects the population of our community?"

Simple concept, complicated answer.

Let's consider first some "answers" that have *not* been successful. In an effort to become diverse, many new clubs have been formed specifically by and for a particular culture, such as a club made up of predominantly Hispanic members, or a club for African Americans, or a club for Muslims, or perhaps a club specifically joined by women.

To be clear, these efforts have succeeded in adding a degree of diversity to Rotary International as a whole. They do not, however, combine the talents and ideology into a club that truly represents the makeup of the entire community.

So, what's the difference?

The ultimate mission and value of having a club with a diverse membership lies in the synergy created when people from different backgrounds form relationships and exchange different perspectives. This provides an enriched club personality and a more complete understanding of the real challenges and needs of their community. The unity and depth of understanding that results at the club level is the ultimate goal for which we strive.

The difficulty of building the diverse club is that it takes personal relationships among the members to make it possible to have that depth of understanding required to serve as a cohesive and unified Rotary club. Further, these relationships take time to develop – often more time than we realize. It also takes a level of commitment from everyone involved according to Stephen Covey who says *"seek first to understand each other, and then to be understood."* It's a give and take endeavor.

It can be far more difficult to introduce different cultures into an existing club with an established persona and character than to build a new club where diversity is an important priority. This is where it becomes important to consider your ultimate objective. Careful study of the community and its demographics prior to the charter of a new club makes it infinitely more likely that you can achieve success at building a club rich in diversity and creativity in the future.

Rotary encourages clubs to assess those in their communities who are eligible for membership under existing membership rules, and to make an effort to reflect their community with regard to professional and business classification, gender, age, religion and ethnicity.

Yet for some, networking with people unlike ourselves is stepping out of our comfort zone. Whether it is our skin color, our religion, our education or our pocketbook, many of us tend to gravitate toward people who remind us of ourselves.

We don't always want to try and understand competing cultural characteristics – but we should. The fact is that each culture has differences in the way members communicate with one another, how they define themselves, how they feel about personal autonomy compared to societal responsibilities, and their attitude about relationships with others.

As an international service organization with clubs in over 200 countries, it is essential that Rotarians learn to deal with two distinct cultural issues:

How do we embrace other cultures outside our club?

Among Rotary International's stated goals are *promoting peace, fighting disease, providing clean water, supporting education* and *growing local economies.* Rotary has a remarkable ability to bring people together. Rotarians are people of action reaching out to third world countries to help solve serious economic, health and social problems. Even the Youth Exchange program has the goal of "making the world smaller."

As Rotarians extend a hand toward other cultures, however, we must understand that the characteristics of each of these countries affect how they do business with, and socially interact with, other cultures.

Some cultures are more family and loyalty focused. They build trust based on relationships and handshakes, while other cultures are more likely to demand written contracts to govern business relationships.

Some are likely to show great respect for older individuals, regardless of their station in life, while others are probably going to need to be convinced of the worthiness of respect, either through education, power or financial gain.

Some look at women in a more traditional manner. Women may not be as respected in the workplace or in a social setting or may be expected to provide traditional duties like serving men, while others demand the same respect a man would receive and would not expect to take on these additional, often subservient, roles.

Other social cues are different in various cultures. For instance, physical closeness by a person from one country might be misinterpreted in another locale as invading his or her personal space, or an attempt at physical intimidation. Likewise, failure to get physically close or to portray immediate social cues of respect in a one country might be misconstrued as arrogance or disrespect in another.

It's not difficult to understand that cultural differences complicate communication between cultures. Further, within each subgroup in a culture will exist variations of beliefs and values. Without an understanding of the basic cultural variances, clubs cannot successfully do business with each other or promote products and services on an international scale.

To partner with Rotary clubs and serve people in other countries, we must make attempts to understand the diverse dimensions from around the world and how they differ in the way they see themselves and interact with others. When we harbor a strong belief that our way of life is the only right way to live, work and raise a family, we are subscribing to a way of thinking that tends to result in a club culture that is judgmental and unforgiving of differing values and beliefs.

How do we embrace other cultures within our club?

Local clubs have to ask themselves, how diverse is my club? How diverse is my community? If the diversity of your community is not reflected in your club, why not?

Do potential members go uninvited because of their race, religion or politics? If so, you are leaving a valuable resource untapped and are missing out on a chance to enrich your life and the life of your club in a way you never imagined.

When we think about diversity in our club, it should not just be a box to check or a percentage to achieve. Instead, in a vibrant club, the want for diversity must be ingrained in its deeply held principles. The club must seek out diversity *with purpose*.

The Rotary International Code tells us that a club's membership should be fully reflective of the community it serves, and that Rotary recognizes the value of diversity within individual clubs.

Don't let your club find itself with a lack of diversity among its own members, begging the question: *How do we bring the world closer if we don't start right here at home?*

One of Rotary International's core values is to connect and serve people throughout the world. By starting with cultural diversity at the local club level, Rotarians are better equipped to make a difference by working to unite people from all continents and cultures to make positive changes around the world.

Have some great ideas about increasing diversity in your local club, please email us, leave a comment on our Facebook page www.facebook.com/PerfectEngagementPublishing or private message us.

CHAPTER 7

Recruiting Younger Members – Less Talk, More Action

"Before you are a leader, success is all about growing yourself. When you become a leader, success is all about growing others."

– Jack Welch

It seems every time a group of Rotarians gather, the subject of recruiting younger members comes up. It's great that we want to talk about it, but what we really need to do is *take action*.

According to the 2013 Regional Membership Supplement published by Rotary International, 71% of members in the United States and Canada are over the age of 50. Only 12% of Rotarians in the U.S. and Canada are younger than 40 years, which Rotary International reports as a worldwide trend.

Why do we care about recruiting younger members anyway? The answer to that is simple. Younger members bring energy, enthusiasm, new ideas and different perspectives.

In addition, younger members provide your club with growth and future sustainability. Think about all the hard work you put into your Rotary club to make it effective and to keep the club's projects going. Think of all the board meetings and the committee meetings and discussions you've had, and all the goals you set for the future of your club.

Now consider what happens to all that hard work when you're gone. If everyone in your Rotary club is roughly the same age, and that age is well over 50, then all the hard work you put into your club will fade away with each passing year. The benefit of recruiting younger members is not only in their fresh ideas, enthusiasm, and new approach to projects, but also in the fact that you have a group of people to carry on your club's work and traditions.

A good place to start recruiting is right in your own backyard, so to speak. What are your grown children doing? Are they in their late 20s and early 30s and in the early stages of their careers? Do you see in them a desire to connect with other business people and a desire to make a difference in the world? These are traits on which you can capitalize, and an opportunity to show them the value of Rotary.

Not all your adult children will have this desire. Their life situation may be different and they may not be at a place where they can take advantage of what Rotary has to offer. But they are still a great resource for you.

Have some serious conversations with your grown children about what people of their generation look for, how they interact with others, how they prefer to work, and what they are hoping to get out of involvement in a civic organization. You may be surprised by what you learn from their answers and the information will be enormously valuable in changing the complexion of your Rotary club.

It's important to remember we are not looking for younger members simply to change the demographic of our clubs or for what they can do for us. Nor are we trying to grow our clubs for the sake of numbers. Don't ignore the fact that you are bringing something of great value to them, as well.

Where else could a professional in their late twenties sit down to breakfast or lunch with the CEO of the local hospital, the superintendent of the local school district, a local elected official, or executives and influential people in your community? The experience is invaluable. They have an opportunity to become friends with these people and to work on projects together, an opportunity they would never have otherwise.

Our good friend and the founding president of our own Rotary club, Andy Eads, had a great idea that he proposed to a neighboring Rotary club. It really speaks to the intentionality of recruiting. This club was in an urban area with several nearby office buildings full of medium to large size companies.

He suggested making visits to the top-level management of the companies to ask them to identify the young, up-and-coming leaders. He further suggested telling the executives about the opportunities of Rotary, and how it is a great platform for these young leaders to learn civic responsibility while building important business relationships in their community. He then recommended they join a local Rotary club.

If a company is behind the idea of their young leaders joining Rotary, especially if they are willing to pay the bill, new generations of Rotarians are easily born.

When we talk about recruiting young people, remember how they must feel when they walk into a room of people who are twenty, thirty or forty years older than themselves. With that in mind, encourage them to invite their friends to be a part of the club. Two or three or more young people will give an immediate boost to your club, and they will feel connected right away.

There's been a great deal of talk lately about new ways to do Rotary, such as reducing the number of meetings each month or having staggered levels of membership. This flexibility is great, but it needs to be balanced with Rotary traditions.

Don't let your enthusiasm for getting young people into your club take you down a road of complete change to the extent you start eliminating Rotary traditions. The traditions are in place for a reason, and as one of our friends likes to remind us, make sure you keep the "Rotary" in Rotary.

These are just a few ideas for getting young people into your club. Remember, you must be intentional when recruiting these members. Don't expect them to seek out your club. They probably have an outdated impression of what a Rotary club is based on their grandfather's experience, and they may even think Rotary is only for older people.

Let's be the ones who dispel this myth!

Recruiting younger members to Rotary is important for many reasons, not the least of which is to groom future generations to embrace a **"Service Above Self"** value system.

CHAPTER 8

The Family of Rotary - Beyond The

Mission Statement

"When I stand before God at the end of my life, I would
hope that I would not have a single bit of talent left,
and could say, 'I used everything you gave me.'"

– Erma Bombeck

Rotary International was founded as *"an international service*
organization whose stated purpose is to bring together
business and professional leaders in order to provide
humanitarian services, encourage high ethical standards in

all vocations, and to advance goodwill and peace around the world."

As such, Rotary remained primarily a business-oriented organization for the first ninety years of its existence. In the mid-nineties, as the desire to develop a more balanced membership that included women and minorities matured, clubs began to realize for the first time that continued growth and success depended on integrating a significant social element.

Prior to modern transportation, family units lived and worked in close proximity to each other. Children were raised with grandparents and cousins, and family members took care of one another. Today, however, it is not uncommon to live in a city or a state located hundreds of miles from our closest relatives. It is also not unusual for family members to be estranged geographically or emotionally, or for a person to have no living relatives at all.

Regardless of a person's constraints, however, the need for community and family still persists. We are a tribal people, always in search of a sense of community and belonging.

For this reason, we often look to our community or organizations to replace or supplement the family bond. That's one of the great things about a Rotarian's family. Like families, Rotary clubs have the ability to be unique in their own way while maintaining their focus on the mission and goals of the organization.

As the baby boomer generation came of age (Americans born from 1946-1964) Rotarians started to place more emphasis on personal relationships with their neighbors, communities and civic organizations. Put another way, Rotarians were wanting to become more socially connected and perform more and more like a family.

So what is family?

Webster's Dictionary gives us multiple definitions of family, including "a group of people united by certain convictions or a common affiliation."

How do you define family?

Hopefully yours is a family of unconditional love where members support each other, celebrating the good things and lending comfort and support when things go wrong. In most families, family members step in and provide support and comfort when an illness or death in the family occurs, or in the event of a tragedy. That same family is there to celebrate the joys in life – birthdays, anniversaries, graduations, births and more.

Reality check.
That's not everyone's family experience.

Each person's understanding of family is different, based on their experiences, and often the meaning of family changes throughout the seasons of our lives.

How do we go about making members into friends and friends into family?

Know that Rotary is a family – made up of people who choose to be family – that promotes and values the family unit of its members. To create a smaller but better world, we must start with family. And we must be a family if we are going to live out our Rotary purpose.

Some easy ways to expand the "family" aspect of your Rotary members are:

1. Have greeters at each meeting reach out a hand or give a hug as members and guests arrive and engage in conversation to help build relationships.

2. Incorporate a "vocational minute" into each meeting to give a different member each week the opportunity to share not just about his or her profession, but also about his or her family, hobbies, or hopes and dreams.

3. Many clubs keep a "happy jar" where members donate money to the Rotary Foundation or a Rotary supported charity in exchange for telling the club

about something that makes them happy or any general news they want to share.

4. Encourage members to break away from their "cliques" regularly to sit with members they don't know well.

5. Several times a year, take a few minutes to play a team building game or have members participate in an exercise to learn more about each other.

A club that makes the effort to build a strong family structure has members with a natural bond and carries out service projects with more energy and passion.

Most Rotary clubs acknowledge their members trials in life at least informally, but your family of Rotary should do more. Consider adopting an official "Family of Rotary" committee from the membership, similar to a benevolence committee commonly found in many churches, to care and nurture those in need.

The act of nurturing and supporting the members of a Rotary club makes a significant and profound difference during times of grief. It builds strong personal relationships and friendships that not only strengthens the membership but serves as a natural way to retain members for years to come.

Support can come in many forms; providing meals for comfort, offering prayers, flowers, heartfelt cards, emails and texts for emotional support, and hospital visitations during times of sickness or the death of a loved one.

When you share in your community or extended family, your problems become shared, as do your joys.

This same sentiment can also be beneficial during times of celebration or great joy. Sharing significant events such as graduations, birthdays, anniversaries and the birth of children or grandchildren.

Having an established program and adequate funding allows members to share both the happiness and the tragedies of all the members of the organization. A stronger recruitment and retention program would be difficult to imagine.

We credit a fellow Rotarian in our home club who is an esteemed psychologist and family counselor in our community for her suggestions in establishing this critical piece. She was instrumental in the development and implementation of our "Family of Rotary" program, and her passion and compassion for our members has been inspirational to us all.

Spend some time developing a strong "Family of Rotary" program. When you reach out to members you make a deposit in their emotional bank. Likewise, when Rotary asks something of its members, a withdrawal is made.

Keep up the deposits to reconcile your members' emotional accounts and ensure they always know their family cares for them. This makes for happy members who are willing to serve the club and the community at the drop of a hat!

CHAPTER 9

Identifying & Empowering Leaders –

Steering the Way to Success

"Leaders don't create followers, they create more leaders."
– Tom Peters

The success or failure of any Rotary club depends on the quality and energy of its leaders.

A well thought out leadership plan will serve your club and build continuity, so choose wisely. The leaders set the tone of the meetings, impact the personality of the membership, create the club culture, and can make or break the ability of the members to achieve the club's mission.

For these reasons, you must have a plan in place to ensure continuity, while at the same time building on the success of previous leaders.

When starting a new club, this plan becomes even more critical. Once you decide on the focus of your new club, put leaders in place who have experience in Rotary – preferably in a leadership role – who can help facilitate that focus.

While it can be done, starting a new club made up entirely of members new to Rotary requires a much greater learning curve than beginning with experienced Rotary leaders.

In a 2015 article, Joe Iarocci blogged that leadership books were published at the rate of more than four per day!

Why are so many books written about leadership?

We can speculate as to why so many leadership books are written, but we believe it's because there are hundreds of different ways to lead and to spot a leader. What we also know is that just because a person is placed in a position of leadership does not necessarily make them a good leader.

"Leadership" can be defined in a multitude of ways, but we think a leader must have the ability to inspire others. In Drew Dudley's Ted Talk *Everyday Leadership*, he says that many people are uncomfortable calling themselves a leader, but he points out that all of us influence people every day, whether we are conscious of it or not. All of us have moments in our lives where something we said or did made another's life fundamentally better. That may be the first step of leadership.

As Rotarians, our ability to serve our community and communities around the world depends on the identification and development of strong, influential leaders. Everyone can think of some of the characteristics of good leaders, but the

Center for Creative Leadership found that great leaders consistently possess these 10 core traits:

- Honesty
- Ability to delegate
- Communication
- Sense of humor
- Confidence
- Commitment
- Positive attitude
- Creativity
- Ability to inspire
- Intuition

We suggest the addition of one more trait: **empathy**. Empathy is the ability to understand and share the feelings of another. Why add empathy? Just look at the Rotary Four-Way Test of the Things We Think, Say or Do.

First, is it the truth? This one is easily measured by honesty. But what about the other three? These call for a good measure of empathy. How do we know if it is fair to all concerned, will build good will and better friendships, and be beneficial to all concerned unless we can attempt to walk in someone else's shoes for a season?

We know some of the characteristics of a good leader, but how do we find those with the greatest potential to be leaders in our club?

Many clubs have traditionally operated on a seniority system. If you stick around long enough, you are likely to become a board member and then eventually the president of your club. While this is not the necessarily the best system, you might actually find some good leaders by default.

Let's look at some other more effective alternatives. We talk about getting younger people in our community involved in Rotary in another chapter, but once we have put their Rotary pin on their lapel, how do we groom them for leadership?

First? Ask them. Yes, it's that simple. Some newer members will be shy about speaking up. They will assume they don't have enough experience or they are not old enough to participate in the policy and decision making of the club.

Rotary, like most other nonprofit organizations and service clubs, is governed by its board of directors. Rather than have the same directors serve year after year, find a way to get some of your young people onto the board.

Don't have enough slots or don't think they know enough? Think about amending your bylaws to allow for some advisory positions or new committee heads. Worried about changing your bylaws or your traditional way of doing things? George Bernard Shaw said, *"Progress is impossible without change, and those who never change their minds never change anything."*

An obvious question: Won't that upset older members who want to stay active on the board and who aren't willing to give up their seat at the table? Not when they understand that leadership succession is all about capitalizing on the experience and wisdom of older members and existing leaders, while at the same time grooming the next generation of leaders.

One idea to consider is to create a "Presidents Leadership Council" made up of all the previous club presidents. The Presidents Leadership Council duties can include tasks such as identifying leaders from the membership, training new board members and committee chairs, and developing the slate of officers and board members for the following year.

The council members can also make themselves available for one-on-one time to mentor the younger members.

A Presidents Leadership Council can benefit the club by utilizing all the knowledge learned by the members from their years of service and their professional and personal wisdom. Further, because they have held positions of leadership in the past, there will be little or no competitive feelings toward newer members who aspire to lead.

Make this transition a fun experience. Graduate previous board members onto the Presidents Leadership Council with ceremony. Present the new members with a special pin or ribbon to celebrate their accomplishments and validate their past service. Like wearing a Paul Harris ribbon and medallion around your neck, a seat on the Presidents Leadership Council should be something to be proud of.

Continually seek to identify and develop qualified members to assume leadership roles who will encourage and inspire your club.

CHAPTER 10

Communications - Is Anyone Listening?

"Tell me and I'll forget. Show me and I might remember. Involve me and I will understand."
— Benjamin Franklin

If a Rotary club is going to engage its members and achieve its goals and objectives, it must have a communication strategy. With no paid employees, communications are typically left to a volunteer administrator, one who may have a limited amount of time and often a limited amount of skill in this area, but is responsible for the tasks associated with getting timely, effective messages to members, the media and other stakeholders.

Likewise, the receiver of the messages are fellow Rotarians busy with jobs and families but volunteering their time to the organization. As a result, a club's communication strategy must be:

* Simple
* Efficient
* Direct
* Easily Accessible

A successful plan will convey the impact and influence of the club members and the organization to the media, local government officials, other service clubs, potential donors and volunteers, as well as the public, to promote community visibility and engagement.

Rotary International, like many other service organizations, was created around the turn of the 20th century during a time of significant changes in the United States related to swift industrialization and the rapid influx of immigrants from around the world.

In addition to Rotary International, other clubs were organized in the early 1900s, including Lions Clubs, Boy Scouts, Knights of Columbus, the Red Cross, the Urban League, Optimists International and Kiwanis. These organizations helped form more solid relationships between service-minded individuals and the communities in which they lived, as well as to contribute to building trust and fellowship among local businessmen. (Remember, this was the early 1900s and service clubs were not for women – yet.)

Within sixteen years of the time Paul Harris created the first Rotary club, sixty clubs had been founded on six continents, an impressive feat considering the lack of speed and efficiency of communications of the time.

Today many of the members of Rotary are seasoned professionals who are extremely busy with their own business of making a living, raising a family, participating in other civic or charitable organizations and being a positive influence on the community. Clubs not only meet weekly, but have constant requests for members to participate in service projects and represent the club at fundraisers and other events. Yet, clubs typically see the participation by members to be lacking, and the same members tend to participate in all the events while others fail to engage in these projects and events in a meaningful way.

The mission of Rotary is *"to provide service to others, promote integrity, and advance world understanding, goodwill, and peace through its fellowship of business, professional, and community leaders."* As a service-based organization, it is *not* okay for many members to reap the benefits offered by the organization but fail to engage fully with the values and requirements of the Rotary motto: **"Service Above Self."**

The real question is:

Does your club efficiently and effectively engage members and other stakeholders in a manner that will gain their attention and compel them to act when called upon?

We recently conducted research in our local club about the current types of communication utilized and the types of communication club members typically respond to and why. The goal was to determine the message style and content that works best so that the club can begin to better communicate with its members and all other stakeholders.

Our club has several committees charged with programs, membership, service projects, financial matters and social aspects of the club, and it must learn how to effectively communicate with each group. Your club likely has the same types of committees and faces the same communication challenges.

One of the primary emphases of a typical Rotary club is the attendance at weekly meetings. According to the Rotary

International policies, clubs should periodically hold regular meetings exclusively for imparting Rotary information, Rotary education, and leadership training to their members.

Unfortunately, we found that many of the messages conveyed at meetings were not reaching every member due to absences and inattention during the meetings. As expected with a large group who enjoy each other's company, members tend to want to visit and often miss important information.

The primary means of communicating information in writing is typically through emails sent to each member. These emails come from club leadership, other members, Rotary International or the District Governor's office. They are delivered through the Clubrunner portal and are immediately recognized as a Rotary communication due to the uniform "look and feel" with few customizable options.

Our research showed overwhelmingly, participants did not read all the emails received and that the amount of information received by email in a given week was just too much.

Members often felt these emails did not contain information which stirred any interest, and as a result, the vast majority of emails from the district level go unread, and many go unopened.

The research further showed that Rotarians want to see no more than one or two written communications per week containing everything they should know about upcoming events. They wanted this communication to be in an easy-to-read, bullet-type format containing only the necessary information.

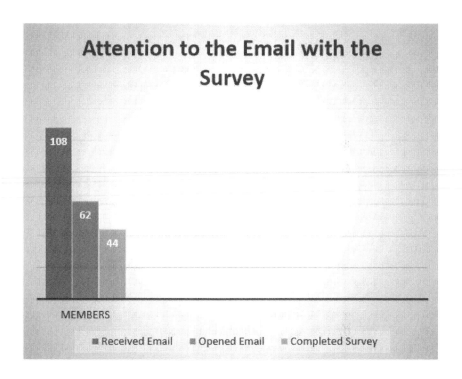

We confirmed this information with a short, mostly quantitative, survey emailed to each member of the club. Prior to sending the email, we notified the members we would be sending them a *completely anonymous three-minute survey.*

Yes, we even warned them in advance and told them it would only take three minutes of their time!

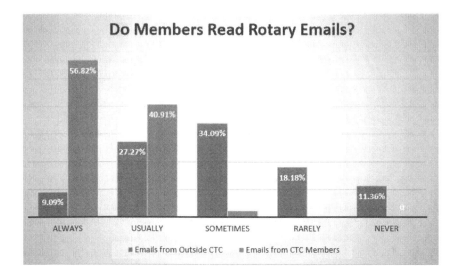

The email with the survey link was sent to all 108 members of our club, with a 100% successful delivery rate. However, after 72 hours, the email was only opened by 62 members – a 58% open rate. More telling, only 44 of the 62 members that opened the email went on to complete the three-minute survey, which translates to a 40% completion rate of all members and a 67.7% completion rate of those who opened the email.

Most surprising to us? A full one-third of the people who opened the email did not take the *three minutes* required to complete the survey!

When asked whether they read Rotary emails from people outside our club, only 9% said they *always* do, while 27% said they *usually* do. Worse news? Almost 20% *rarely* read Rotary emails and 11% *never* read them at all.

However, when asked about whether they read emails from fellow club members, over half the members said they always read them, and another 40% said they usually do.

The takeaway? Approximately 42% of our members do not even open many Rotary emails! While we can't assume this statistic is true in every club, it merits notice and is not likely limited to our club.

It is safe to say that a large amount of communications sent by Rotary clubs do not reach their recipients in an effective way. Instead, many messages go unread by members.

So what does work?

We found a better way to grab Rotarians' attention is through group texts and social media messages directed toward members. While this may not prove to be true in your club, we know that social media and other forms of group communication is here to stay. Why not give it a try?

Social media is so important that we have devoted an entire chapter to it. In case you doubt it's value, as of 2017, approximately 67% of Americans stated they utilize social media as a means of at least some of their news consumption. The number of users has continued to grow since the emergence of social media and the relevance of social strategies for service organizations is obvious.

- Facebook has been identified as the largest source of news gathering by people living in the United States.

- Among Twitter users, 74% of adults in the United States said that they get their news from the app.

- Instagram has more than 800 million monthly active users.

Facebook – Twitter – Instagram. Start using it!

There are many group texting applications available for free use. Groupme, Whatsapp and Slack are just a few options that offer free group texting, and chances are, by the time this book is distributed there will be many more. These applications can be used by individual committees and social groups to send text communications, photographs and videos to other members of the group.

Willmon White, an editor of *The Rotarian*, once said, *"All human institutions, like humans themselves, grow, change, adapt, reinvent themselves – or they tend to wither and die."*

To avoid withering and dying, Rotary clubs must change their communication strategy and continue to evolve with technology and with the habits of their members.

CHAPTER 11

Public Relations & Social Media – Thriving in the 21st Century

"We don't have a choice on whether we DO social media, the questions is how well we DO it."
– Erik Qualman

Here we are, well into the 21st century. We have experienced a whirlwind of advancement in the world of technology, and all the good and bad that goes along with it.

The question is, has your club embraced it?

The use of social media in service organizations like Rotary can not only build and maintain relationships with stakeholders but can positively affect the revenues. Used effectively, social media can help your club better communicate with and engage your members, but will also help your club reach potential members, volunteers and donors.

Whether or not you are a fan of social media and the literal "worldwide" exposure you are offered, the time is now to embrace it. That's right, no more worrying about whether you are doing it right or saying too much or putting the wrong thing out there – it's time to get started!

Some of you who are reading this are experts, or at least quite proficient, at all things promotional and social media related. That's a great gift! But many continue to be hesitant about dipping their toe into the self-promotion waters, even for their own Rotary club.

Our first bit of advice is to start with what is offered at no charge. And while this paragraph may be obsolete a year from now, we'll say it anyway. Start by building a Facebook page. It sounds simple, we know, but many Rotary clubs continue to fall short, for many reasons. Let's talk about a few.

If you are afraid you will "do it wrong," don't be. It's almost foolproof. You must start somewhere and getting your club name out there is the first step.

If you are concerned about privacy issues, don't be. You are building an organizational page, and personal risk and exposure is minimal, if at all. You want enough information on the page to let people find you, but that won't include entering personal details for the world to see.

If you are worried you won't know what to do once you have the page set up, don't be. The fun of having a presence on social media is that it creates a *buzz* about your organization, and you will start to see things that need to be promoted everywhere you turn once you have this mindset. Also it might be a great job for one of those younger members you are recruiting.

If you don't want to use Facebook because you've heard it's losing participants, or that young people don't use it, put that out of your mind. No matter how many people tell you they are leaving the Facebook world, it continues to be exponentially larger in scope and audience than all other social media platforms. And while it's true that your teenage children or grandchildren are not using Facebook, young professionals still are. Your message needs to be where the people are!

If you have already taken this first step, great! Let's talk about using it to its fullest.

You may be hesitant to post anything on social media because it just doesn't seem important enough. You're waiting for the big fundraising gala or your club's 25th anniversary celebration to post. Or you have limited your posts to the upcoming speakers or to your Paul Harris recipients.

Those are great instances to promote your club if you use your Facebook page like a club newsletter. But the true value of social media is what it can do for growing your membership and building visibility and support in your community on a regular basis.

Although a post that includes 65 photos from your recent gala is fun for your club members to scroll through and serves as a mini photo album of the night, it means little to most of the world. That's not to take away from the obvious benefit of having a page your members can enjoy; it's just not the main objective of social media promotion.

Try taking your social media to the next level and start using your posts as a way to reach out to people who might not be familiar with your club or might not have ever heard of Rotary or its mission.

Show the world the important work you do and how much fun you have doing it.

**Social media is all about
Exposure, Exposure, Exposure.**

Think of the impact of two or three photos of happy, smiling faces at a weekly meeting, or a picture of a group of smiling Rotarians working on a service project, or a photo of your visitors to the meeting one week. The pictures alone draw you in and make you want to be a part of what's going on!

But even though "a picture is worth a thousand words," DON'T FORGET THE WORDS. Be sure and give a one or two sentence description of what's happening in the picture and identify and "tag" the people. Use the "check-in" feature whenever you can, just so you are connected to as many different people, places and businesses as possible.

Adapt the saying (that we made up) that "no good deed goes un-promoted." We say it for a reason, because everything you do as a club, or a member does on behalf of your club, should be celebrated and shared.

Consider a Twitter account, which is an easy way to push out club information to members and other stakeholders. An Instagram account is another fun and easy way to share photographs of club activities. These are the next two largest social media platforms, so don't be afraid to give them a try.

Be sure to "like" and "follow" Rotary International, as well as other Rotary clubs. You will get great ideas for future posts and you are guaranteed to learn more about Rotary in the process. Also, make sure you "share" your club's posts onto your personal page. These small things will dramatically increase your club's exposure and effectiveness.

Finally, don't overlook the power of traditional media.

Contrary to popular belief, newspaper are *not* dead. While many still print, and many communities still depend on that – they almost all have an online presence, as well. That online "newspaper" story quickly becomes a social media post that can be shared to your club's page. It's the perfect way to hold onto the tradition of a good, old-fashioned newspaper article while embracing technology and using it to get that story out to the world.

A relationship with the local newspaper, magazine, or social media professional is a valuable asset to help get the accomplishments and projects of a club in front of the public and certainly gets the attention of prospective members.

The ultimate goal of your promotional efforts with any social media platform is to drive traffic to your website. Your website is where potential members and current members alike can find detailed information about your club – officers, history, meeting time and location, membership information, upcoming projects, and more – and it is the place where your club's personality can shine.

Consider developing a plan for your club to expand its message to members, the media, volunteers and donors. Here are a few tips:

1. **Keep it Short.** Members are busy with family and professional commitments, so the messages need to be short and to the point.

2. **Keep it Dynamic.** Rather than lining up a group of people for a photo in front of a wall, catch the subject or subjects in action, showing their enthusiasm and personality.

3. **Keep it Consistent.** Every message on social should reinforce your club's – and Rotary's – ideals and

mission. Use the same words and phrases to build the brand. Whether in person, at a meeting, in an email or Facebook post, stay on topic and repeat it often. As an example, every member, potential member, donor, beneficiary or other contact needs to know that **"Service Above Self"** is synonymous with your Rotary Club.

4. **Keep it Current.** If you have a Facebook page, you must be consistent in your posting frequency. Post several times each week and keep the content fresh and varied.

5. **Keep it (S)Tweet.** Consider the use of Twitter to raise an awareness of club activities to potential members, sponsors, donors and the community in general.

6. **Keep it Real.** Consider starting a blog to be shared on your website and on social media. Sharing content by blogging on an organization's site and on other sites is a great way to grow an audience. Think about allowing individuals to share their experiences about events, groups, programs and the club in general with each other at meetings and on social media.

We are quite certain that Paul Harris did not have social media, or the internet for that matter, in mind when he started Rotary. If he could have imagined even a fraction of its impact he would have been a genius, or possibly considered crazy. But what he did know is that the world is changing, and Rotary must change with it, saying,

"If Rotary is to survive into the future it must change faster than change itself."

Paul Harris knew that while the story of Rotary and its beginning was a compelling one, that story would be continually rewritten to maintain relevance in our ever-changing world.

This is the state of self-promotion now, but we can only imagine how it will evolve. Stay flexible and keep up with the changes. Your club will be the beneficiary of your efforts – stronger, bigger and more effective.

Do you want to learn more tips about how to use the different social media platforms to promote your club? Contact us at letstalk@PerfectEngagementPublishing.com.

A Case Study

Cross Timbers Rotary

"We don't shame or tease people for missing meetings, we stress perfect engagement over perfect attendance."

— Andy Eads

For about a year, several of us who were members of the Flower Mound Rotary Club had been talking about starting a new Rotary club in the area. The Flower Mound Rotary Club is an established club with a membership that hovers between fifty and sixty members. Chartered in 1988, the club meets for lunch every Thursday and features an impressive array of business professionals from the community and a wonderful track record of fundraising events.

Our Assistant Governor at the time, Gerald Robinson, had placed a priority on expanding the footprint of Rotary in Denton County. Two members of the Flower Mound Rotary Club, then Denton County Commissioner Andy Eads and his Chief Administrator Lori Fickling, had been talking about this for months and felt the time might be right to add another club to the area.

A phone call to the District Governor Nominee, Mary Ann McDuff, was the final encouragement needed, and it looked like this new club might actually happen.

Andy and Lori assembled four others plus themselves for an initial founders meeting. Five of the founders were current Rotarians at the Flower Mound Rotary Club, and the other was a spouse whose grandparents had been very active in Rotary in her hometown.

The six founders began to set in motion the groundwork for starting a new club that would become the Cross Timbers Rotary Club.

After several months of careful thought and consideration about exactly how we wanted to craft this new club to make it fun and energetic and easily accessible to new members, a plan was developed.

Because we were basically starting from scratch, we were able to decide on the best day of the week and the best time of day to meet, as well as the "personality" we wanted for our new club. We chose Friday mornings at 8:00 a.m., which would accomplish several important goals.

First, everyone is in a good mood on Fridays and this seemed like the perfect time to get together and have fun with friends as we all head into the weekend. The second important note is that the 8:00 a.m. start time allowed the parents of young children, many of whom take kids to school in the mornings, to be a part of the club after dropping off kids. This is a critical detail when thinking about the makeup of your club.

Due in great part to this one strategic decision, our Cross Timbers Rotary Club membership is made up of 51% women, and has been from the start. In addition, 22% of our members are under the age of 50.

Another important detail was our decision to hold the meetings in a light, bright space that was roomy and nice, and above all, had good food! We really hoped to exchange the "weekly business meeting" feel that plagues many Rotary meetings for an upbeat friendly atmosphere.

From the beginning, we had one major defining criteria for membership in this new club – NO DRAMA. We decided we wanted to foster a club culture of friendship and support with service-minded men and women who enjoyed each other and had a heart to do good in the community and in the world.

The very first meeting of the newly formed Cross Timbers Rotary Club was in late May of 2015, with nineteen prospective members in attendance. The founders set about completing all the paperwork and meeting all the requirements to obtain a charter from Rotary International. We developed committees, chose a board of directors, named officers, and began the serious work of recruiting more members.

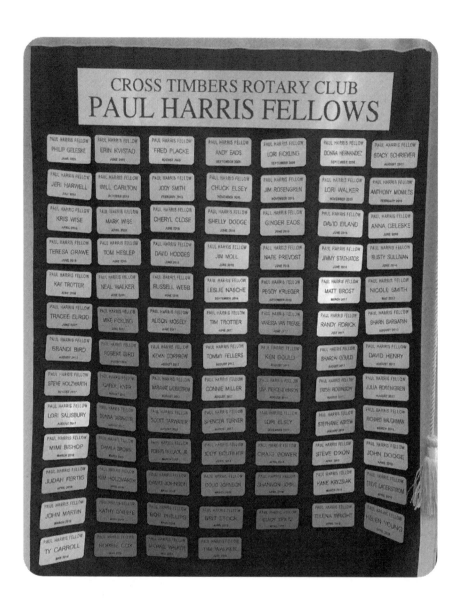

One of the first things we did was to brainstorm a list of what we wanted this club to look like. A good old-fashioned flip chart and markers did the trick. Everyone had a voice in the direction we wanted the club to go.

The second thing on our to-do list was to begin the process of recruiting potential members. This is where everyone's mobile phone came into play. During the first few meetings everyone took out their phone and began scrolling through their contact list. "Look for people you would like to have breakfast or lunch with," the members were told.

And thus began the process.

The lists submitted by each member were delivered to the board who looked for duplicates and eliminated a few suggestions who were just not a good fit. (See the defining principle of NO DRAMA.)

After the lists were "scrubbed," our members and our board began the invitation process. The invites were mostly extended face-to-face or done by a personal phone call. An email invitation or a text message proved less effective, especially since we placed a priority on engagement with potential members with a personal touch.

And as it turns out, not surprisingly, people really want to be invited and included in something special. It's much easier to extend a deliberate invitation than to just hope someone discovers your club and wants to become a member.

As invitations were accepted and lunch appointments were made, the results began to flood in. After all, most of the lunch dates were taking place between close friends and out of a strong sense of respect and sincerity. The intention was to honor the selected prospects and to allow them the opportunity to ask questions about the goals and objectives of the organization. These meetings were casual and highly personal, as well as professional and welcoming.

Another critical action was to specifically recruit members who would broaden the diversity of the membership as a whole. In short, to "recruit with the end in mind." With each meeting that summer, the attendance steadily grew. As a result, so did the membership. Paperwork was submitted, and a major push was in place to recruit "charter members."

When the chartering ceremony took place in late August that year, we chartered with 62 members! Considering our goal had been 50 members, this accomplishment astonished even the founders. The process took many months to develop, but the diligence and the disciplined process yielded incredible results.

With the charter members in place, the process of growing the Cross Timbers Rotary Club began. It was important to us to honor the traditions of Rotary, while at the same time embracing some new traditions of our own.

From the beginning, we made a conscious effort to be active on social media. We immediately created a Facebook page and began posting about all the great fun we were having each week and the service projects we were already involved in. Facebook also served as an effective way to identify people who might be interested in joining our club. In fact, several saw us on Facebook first and reached out to inquire about membership.

The result of this type of recruitment was that from the beginning, 75% of the members of Cross Timbers Rotary had never been in Rotary before. That statistic still holds true today, as members continue to recruit friends and business associates who have never been exposed to the ideals of Rotary.

Our club committed to hosting a foreign exchange student that first year, which proved to be the first of many, and we also committed to place a priority on Foundation giving and awarding Paul Harris Fellows.

A new tradition to encourage Rotary Foundation giving is for our members to deposit a check into our weekly Happy Jar on their birthday week in an amount equal to their age. This is purely voluntary, but it benefits the Rotary Foundation, and as we round out our third year, an impressive 87% of our Rotarians have earned Paul Harris Fellowships.

As this book goes to print, club membership has grown to 108 members, with no signs of slowing down. Members consistently say their hour at Rotary is one of the most uplifting hours of their week, and they are truly sad when they must miss a meeting.

Another important aspect of the club is that we make sure every single member has a job to do. Every duty is broken down into the smallest detail, and each member is assigned a task. Some are weekly, some are monthly, and some are done as needed. But each job is done with enthusiasm and every member feels valued.

One of the most common remarks from our membership has to do with the quality of the speakers and programs they are exposed to each week. It is difficult to overstate the value of consistently inspiring, informative and relevant information presented by the speakers at our weekly meetings, keeping the full attention of the membership and conveying a high degree of respect and appreciation to the speakers. Cross Timbers Rotary is fortunate to have a single point of contact who schedules and coordinates all the programs. She is highly organized, well known throughout the community, and supremely dedicated to her extended Rotary family.

To kick start the mindset of service projects, one of the first things we implemented was a service project that could be done on site during the hour-long Rotary meeting. The first one was stuffing backpacks for underprivileged children who have no food to eat on the weekends when they are not in school. We coordinated with a local nonprofit for a list of preferred contents, and when the project was done the backpacks were delivered to the organization to be distributed at the schools.

This began a tradition of on-site service projects, which is now mixed with many offsite projects, as well, and makes for a very involved club membership. Rotarians are encouraged to bring their children when school is out, which provides the perfect meeting to do a hands-on project and to start instilling the value of Rotary in our children at an early age.

It is also a great opportunity to involve the members of the Interact Club from the local high school by allowing them the chance to work directly with the adult members of the club. Yet another recruiting opportunity for the future of Rotary!

The same theory held true for fundraising. An idea we brought with us from our previous club was one of a silent auction to raise money for our international projects, again done on site during the one hour of Rotary. Members bring an item to donate, and the bidding begins when Rotary starts. Most of the items are on the silent auction portion, but one or two special items inevitably become auctioned in a live auction. As it would happen, our club has a member who's an auctioneer, so this is especially fun!

It is interactive activities like this that build strong personal relationships among our members.

A new club tradition that was the brainstorm of one of our founders is Rotary Action Days, which we refer to as "RAD." Over a 48-hour period each year, our members work in groups to perform community service for our local nonprofits in projects ranging from painting a youth center, working a local clothes closet and helping with an Easter Egg hunt for families in crisis. During our most recent RAD weekend we were able to accomplish 12 service projects!

There is nothing like getting your hands dirty alongside fellow club members to get to know each other. Let the bonding begin!

Cross Timbers Rotary also aggressively encourages every member to be a part of a club sponsored social "fellowship." Options include Rotary Readers, Rotary Campers, Rotary Wine Lovers, Rotary Cruisers and Rotary Chefs, with new ideas welcome as members identify other members with common interests.

The goal is to develop personal relationships with other members who share hobbies, and these grow organically from the interests of club members. The results have been remarkable and have created a sense of excitement that carries over to the regular weekly meetings. These "fellowships" go a long way in all but eliminating the challenge of retaining members.

The Cross Timbers Rotary Club in Flower Mound, Texas, has enjoyed tremendous success as we approach our third anniversary, now 108 members strong. We credit visionary leadership and a carefully crafted plan as the primary reasons.

As a result, about a year and a half in, we were featured in the July 2017 issue of The Rotarian magazine – in an article called Rising Star – with an impressive eight-page full color spread.

Is our story the only way to build a vibrant engaging Rotary Club? Absolutely not. But we hope it shows you one way your group can go from start-up to shifting gears seamlessly into growth mode, while maintaining your momentum, energy and hope for a bright future.

Whether you are interested in starting a new Rotary club or need to breathe new life into your existing club, feel free to reach out to us through our website. We are always happy to share our experiences.

In the meantime, learn how new technology can be your best asset and embrace it. There is no need to re-invent the wheel, but it is necessary to understand how to engage with existing and prospective members to be successful in this 21st century world.

Getting Started

A few questions to get you thinking about your own club and areas that may need attention:

What do you like most about your Rotary Club?

What is one thing you would change about your Rotary Club?

What is your favorite Rotary sponsored activity or project?

Does your Rotary Club have a project that's been around for years but could benefit from being reevaluated?

What is your preferred method of communication with other Rotary Members?

Does your club have a page on Facebook? Are you connected with your club and Rotary International through Facebook?

Are you currently in a leadership position in your club? If not, what position do you feel you are best suited for?

Donna Hernandez

Donna Hernandez is a past president of the Flower Mound Rotary Club and a charter member of the Cross Timbers Rotary Club, where she serves on the Presidents Leadership Council. She founded and published a local weekly direct mail newspaper that quickly grew to a regional media outlet and was purchased by a large national publishing group. Donna is a licensed attorney and holds a M.A. in Strategic Communication & Innovation. She resides in Flower Mound, Texas, with her husband Tommy Hernandez and serves as the administrator for the non-profit Dallas Tigers Baseball Club, Inc.

Lori Fickling

Lori Fickling is a 25-year Rotarian and a founder and past president of the Cross Timbers Rotary Club in Flower Mound, Texas. She was previously president of the Flower Mound Rotary Club and is currently an Assistant Governor in District 5790. Lori and her husband Mike, along with coauthor Donna Hernandez, owned and operated a bi-weekly community newspaper for six years, where she served as both writer and editor. Lori is the President/CEO of the Lewisville Area Chamber of Commerce and social media specialist. She has a B.B.A. from the University of North Texas and lives in Double Oak, Texas with her husband Mike.

Mike Fickling

Mike Fickling is a retired Lewisville, Texas, Firefighter/ Paramedic whose passion is writing. He is a charter member of the Cross Timbers Rotary Club and oversees the club's Rotary Responders program, providing emergency assistance to families who find themselves in immediate and urgent need. Mike owned and operated a community newspaper with his wife, Lori, and friend Donna Hernandez. Mike is a realtor and lives with his wife in Double Oak, Texas. They have three children, a son-in-law, and three grandchildren.

To get in touch with Donna, Lori and Mike for more information about starting or growing a Rotary club, to have them speak at your club or organization, or for quantity book purchases visit:

www.PerfectEngagementPublishing.com

or send an email to:

letstalk@PerfectEngagementPublishing.com

Also please follow us on our social media sites:

www.facebook.com/PerfectEngagementPublishing